# THE RIGHT TO COUNSEL

Titles in the

# Famous Court Cases That Became Movies

series

## The *Amistad* Mutiny

*From the Court Case
to the Movie*

ISBN-13: 978-0-7660-3054-1

ISBN-10:     0-7660-3054-7

## The *Bounty* Mutiny

*From the Court Case
to the Movie*

ISBN-13: 978-0-7660-3128-9

ISBN-10:     0-7660-3128-4

## Presidential Power
## on Trial

*From Watergate to*
All the President's Men

ISBN-13: 978-0-7660-3058-9

ISBN-10:     0-7660-3058-X

## Racism on Trial

*From the Medgar Evers
Murder Case to*
Ghosts of Mississippi

ISBN-13: 978-0-7660-3059-6

ISBN-10:     0-7660-3059-8

## The Right to Counsel

*From* Gideon *v.* Wainwright
*to* Gideon's Trumpet

ISBN-13: 978-0-7660-3057-2

ISBN-10:     0-7660-3057-1

## Witchcraft on Trial

*From the Salem Witch Hunts
to* The Crucible

ISBN-13: 978-0-7660-3055-8

ISBN-10:     0-7660-3055-5

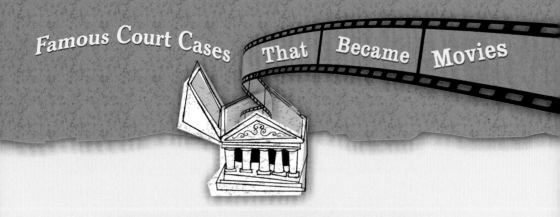

# Famous Court Cases That Became Movies

# THE RIGHT TO COUNSEL

From
*Gideon*
*v.*
*Wainwright*
to
*Gideon's*
*Trumpet*

Lisa Wroble

**Enslow Publishers, Inc.**
40 Industrial Road
Box 398
Berkeley Heights, NJ 07922
USA

http://www.enslow.com

*For my father, who triggered my interest in legal history. Thanks for the great debates!*

**Library of Congress Cataloging-in-Publication Data**

Wroble, Lisa A.
  The right to counsel : from Gideon v. Wainwright to Gideon's trumpet / Lisa
    Wroble.
    p. cm. — (Famous court cases that became movies)
  Summary: "Examines the Supreme Court case Gideon v. Wainwright, including the
    trial and appeals, the ruling of a defendant's right to counsel, and the movie
    inspired by the court case"—Provided by publisher.
  Includes bibliographical references and index.
  ISBN-13: 978-0-7660-3057-2
  ISBN-10: 0-7660-3057-1
    1. Gideon, Clarence Earl—Trials, litigation, etc.—Juvenile literature.  2. Right to
  counsel—United States.  I. Title.
  KF224.G475W76 2009
  345.73'056—dc22

                                               2008017419

Printed in the United States of America

9 8 7 6 5 4 3 2 1

**To Our Readers:**
We have done our best to make sure all Internet addresses in this book were active and appropriate when we went to press. However, the author and the publisher have no control over and assume no liability for the material available on those Internet sites or on other Web sites they may link to. Any comments or suggestions can be sent by e-mail to comments@enslow.com or to the address on the back cover.

♻ Enslow Publishers, Inc., is committed to printing our books on recycled paper. The paper in every book contains 10% to 30% post-consumer waste (PCW). The cover board on the outside of each book contains 100% PCW. Our goal is to do our part to help young people and the environment too!

**Illustration Credits:** AP/Wide World, pp. 6, 27, 71 (bottom), 86; Everett Collection, pp. 3, 13, 67, 71 (top and middle), 75, 77; Collection of the Supreme Court of the United States, p. 50; Collection of the Supreme Court of the United States/Harris and Ewing, pp. 46, 54; Fabian Bachrach/Collection of the Supreme Court of the United States, p. 39; Florida State Archives, p. 21; Getty Images, p. 32; Hessler Studios/Collection of the Supreme Court of the United States, p. 62; Shutterstock, p. 11; Courtesy of Stetson University School of Law, p. 44.

**Cover Illustrations:** Gavel—Digital Stock; courthouse logo—Artville; movie still of Henry Fonda in *Gideon's Trumpet*—Everett Collection.

# CONTENTS

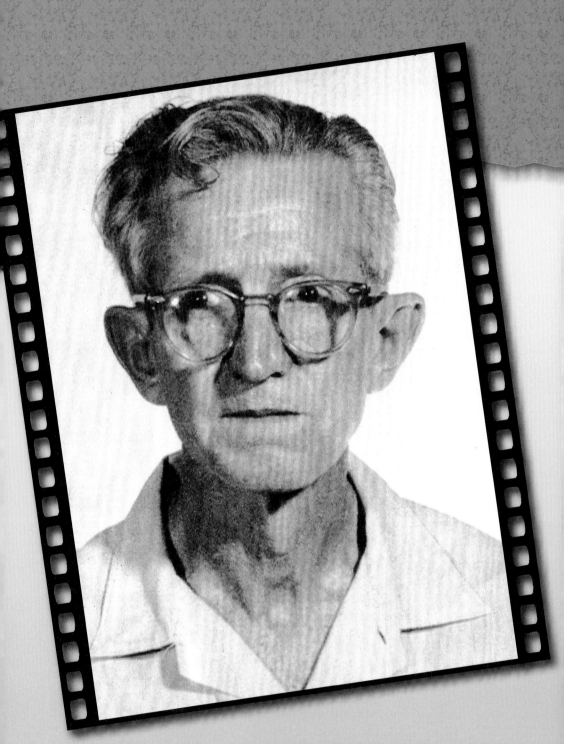

Clarence Earl Gideon, an unemployed drifter, changed the course of U.S. legal history.

# Chapter 1

# Confronting the Court

On a June night in 1961, a Panama City, Florida, deputy was making his rounds. He noticed the door ajar at the Bay Harbor Pool Room. Taking a closer look, the officer saw signs of forced entry. He radioed his findings from his car. Then he questioned a man standing near the corner of the building. The man, Henry Cook, said he had seen Clarence Gideon inside the pool hall. Cook explained that he then had seen Gideon exit the building through a rear door with a bottle of wine and his pockets bulging. He described how he had seen Gideon use the pay phone and then wait until a taxi picked him up.

Investigation of the pool hall revealed a broken window and two vending machines pried open. About

$65.00 in coins was missing, along with some food, cigarettes, and a bottle of wine. Police looked for Gideon and located him at a bar. He was questioned and searched. Finding $25.28 in dimes, nickels, quarters, and a few pennies in his pockets, the police arrested him for the robbery.[1]

## A Man Accused

On August 4, 1961, Clarence Earl Gideon sat in the Panama City courthouse. A drifter with an eighth-grade education, Gideon was familiar with trials and the inside of a courtroom. He had many previous arrests for minor crimes and felonies. He had been convicted and sentenced to prison at least four times. And he supported himself through gambling, mainly by running card games. This time, however, he declared his innocence.

The case on the docket, *State of Florida* v. *Gideon*, charged the defendant with breaking and entering with the intent to commit a larceny. The value of the items taken was under one hundred dollars, which normally would have made the crime a misdemeanor in the state of Florida. However, the charge included breaking in, which was a felony. A guilty verdict would result in prison time for Gideon.

Judge Robert L. McCrary, Jr., of Bay County circuit court, began Gideon's trial before a jury of six men. The judge asked the prosecuting attorney, the lawyer representing the state of Florida against Gideon, whether he was ready for trial. William Harris, assistant state attorney, stated he was. When the judge asked whether Gideon was prepared, Gideon said he was not. He asked for a lawyer because, he said, he could not afford to hire one. According to the court transcript for *State of Florida v. Gideon* (1961), Judge McCrary could not initially understand what Gideon said. The judge told Gideon to approach the bench. The conversation continued:

> THE COURT (Judge McCrary): Now tell us what you said again, so we can understand you please.
>
> DEFENDANT (Gideon): Your Honor, I said: I request this Court to appoint counsel to represent me at this trial.
>
> THE COURT: Mr. Gideon, I am sorry, but I cannot appoint counsel to represent you in this case. Under the laws of the state of Florida, the only time the court can appoint counsel to represent a defendant is when that person is charged with a capital offense. I am sorry, but I have to deny your request to appoint counsel to defend you in this case.
>
> DEFENDANT: The United States Supreme Court says that I am entitled to be represented by counsel.[2]

McCrary said to the court recorder, whose job it is to take notes on everything said and later type a transcript of the proceedings, "Let the record show," and he then summarized the above conversation.[3] Gideon had no choice but to defend himself. He was not given additional time to prepare his case. The trial continued as scheduled.

"Like thousands of people accused of a crime in Florida and elsewhere, Mr. Gideon had been required to go to trial alone. And like thousands, he had done his best, but it wasn't good enough," states a tribute to Gideon by the Connecticut Division of Public Defender Services.[4]

## Right to an Attorney Varied by State

During Gideon's first trial, he asked for a lawyer because he couldn't afford one. Judge McCrary refused. Gideon insisted the Constitution gave him the right to counsel. He referred to the Sixth Amendment, which spells out the rights of anyone accused: "In all criminal prosecutions, the accused shall enjoy the right to a speedy and public trial, by an impartial jury . . . and to have the Assistance of Counsel for his defence."[5]

Originally, this was understood to apply to those accused of a federal charge. Over time, states had made laws that provided for counsel in criminal trials in state court.[6] In 1961, Florida provided counsel for those who could not afford to hire an attorney only for capital crimes. Florida was among thirteen states to interpret the Sixth Amendment in this way.[7] An exception was made if the defendant was a young adult, illiterate, mentally defective, or showed some other special circumstance.[8] Other states offered assistance to poor defendants even in noncapital charges.

In 1942 a case, *Betts* v. *Brady*, came before the Supreme Court with similar details to Gideon's case. Betts was a man accused of robbery who felt he had been denied a fair trial due to lack of counsel. Like Gideon, he had represented himself and was found guilty. Like Gideon, he petitioned the Supreme Court to review his case.

The Supreme Court ruling in *Betts* supported the belief that a layman could have a fair trial without a lawyer, especially in a relatively simple and straightforward case.[9] Both Betts's and Gideon's cases were considered straightforward by the judges who presided over the trials.

The U.S. Supreme Court building. Clarence Earl Gideon, an unemployed drifter, was able to pursue justice in the nation's highest court.

## Changing the Course of Criminal Justice

A determined man, Gideon held firmly to his belief that he had been entitled to an attorney. He would not give up this notion. The *Gideon* trials were the result. They cover three cases beginning in 1961 and concluding with a retrial mandated by the U.S. Supreme Court in 1963. Before that, there were differences in the handling of capital cases (in which a verdict of guilty might involve a life sentence or the death penalty) and noncapital cases. In capital cases, lawyers were automatically appointed for defendants who were too poor to hire their own attorneys. But in noncapital cases, each state determined when to provide an attorney to a defendant who could not afford one.

In the *Gideon* trials, the key factor was that the accused, Clarence Earl Gideon, was convinced the Constitution of the United States guaranteed him a lawyer when he asked for one. Though he did not fully understand the law, his determination caused him to take pencil in hand and do something about his situation. His action changed the course of criminal justice in this country.

While in prison, Gideon wrote to the Supreme Court, expressing his belief that his rights for due process of law, as provided for in the Fourteenth Amendment to the Constitution, had been violated by Florida courts. The Supreme Court listened.

The result of *Gideon* v. *Wainwright* (1963) was a landmark ruling. It ensured that the accused in every state had the right to an attorney in felony cases whether they could afford one or not.

The actor Henry Fonda portrayed Gideon in the TV movie
made about the landmark case, *Gideon's Trumpet*.

## What About Miranda Rights?

Anyone who watches television shows about police or lawyers knows the accused have rights—especially the right to a lawyer. Charges get dropped if police do not "read the rights" when someone is arrested. But Gideon did not ask for a lawyer when he was arrested, because that law had not yet been created. The Miranda warning is something we take for granted today. Its purpose is to advise the accused of their rights. But it did not become a law until 1966.

Actually, the *Gideon* trials became important stepping stones toward clarifying these rights. The *Gideon* trials raised questions. Some were answered during these trials. Others were answered later, such as "When is the accused entitled to a lawyer?" In 1961, the law said Gideon could hire a lawyer. Since he could not afford one, the law said the judge could decide when and if Gideon should get a free, court-appointed lawyer.

## The Movie: *Gideon's Trumpet*

A year after the Supreme Court ruling allowing Clarence Gideon a new trial with the aid of counsel, Anthony Lewis published a book, *Gideon's Trumpet*. Lewis was a columnist for *The New York Times* who had worked in the newspaper's Washington bureau covering the Supreme Court and the Justice Department. The book told the story of Gideon's ordeal. In 1980, a television movie was made based on Lewis's book.

Henry Fonda portrays Clarence Earl Gideon as a man aged beyond his years due to a hard life but firm in his convictions and undeterred by the hard luck that led him to prison. He is set on proving his innocence. He believes strongly in the rights granted by the Consti-tution—that all men have the right to due process of law—and that because he was denied an attorney when he requested one, he had not received proper due process.

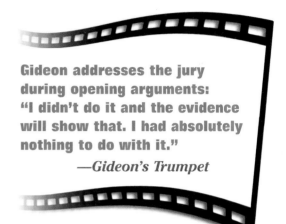

Gideon addresses the jury during opening arguments: "I didn't do it and the evidence will show that. I had absolutely nothing to do with it."
—*Gideon's Trumpet*

The movie portrays the difference one poor, under-educated man can have through belief in convictions and the framework of our government—the U.S. Constitution.

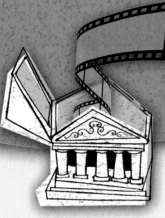

# Chapter 2

# Alone and on Trial

Gideon made his best attempt to show his innocence. Though he might have been through trials before, he had no law training. He blundered through the motions and attempted to play the part of a lawyer. But he was unable to examine witnesses effectively. When he asked the chief eyewitness, Henry Cook, about his criminal record, the prosecutor objected. Judge McCrary explained that Gideon couldn't ask such a question.[1]

## What Testimony Revealed

Cross-examination is intended to find omissions or inconsistencies in the testimony of the witness. Gideon's attempts to cross-examine the chief eyewitnesses, Henry Cook and Irene Rhodes, went nowhere.

Cook's answers provided no further information aside from the fact that he claimed to have seen Gideon inside the poolroom and saw him leave through the rear door with a bottle of wine. Rhodes, a woman sitting on her porch on the night of the crime, testified that she had seen Gideon emerge from the alley behind the poolroom and walk to the telephone booth with a bottle of wine. She saw the taxi pick him up. Both Cook and Rhodes knew Gideon.

The purpose of a witness should have been to provide facts in favor of his defense. Gideon called the taxi driver and the police officer who arrested him. He even called his former landlady, who answered questions regarding Gideon's character. She testified that he was not the type to get drunk and verified that he often used the pay phone outside the pool hall during the night to avoid disturbing the other boarders.[2] Such ineffective questioning of witnesses illustrated Gideon's method for defense.[3]

The most incriminating testimony, or the statement that worked most against Gideon, came from the taxi driver who picked Gideon up the night of June 3, 1961. He testified that Gideon said, upon getting into the cab, that if anyone asked, "You haven't seen me."[4] This statement seemed to show Gideon's secrecy—and guilt.[5] A lawyer might have tried to clarify that statement through redirect testimony—or questioning this witness again after cross-examination. However, Clarence Gideon did not.

Throughout the trial, he attempted to present his good moral character and to show himself innocent of the charges against him.

## What Is Due Process?

Due process is the idea that laws and legal proceedings must be fair. The Constitution says that no U.S. citizen can lose the right to life, liberty, or property without due process of law. If a private citizen tries to take away these rights, a person can take legal action. The government cannot take away a person's basic rights either, without due process—namely a fair trial. A guilty verdict in a case with a death penalty would violate due process if it was arrived at without first having a fair trial. Being sent to prison would deny liberty without a fair trial.

### The Sad Result

Judge McCrary tried to gently guide Gideon through court protocol. But Gideon continued to fumble through the trial. When Gideon rose to state his closing remarks, for example, he was informed that the prosecutor goes first. The prosecutor summarized the facts and eyewitness testimony while Gideon restated his innocence.[6]

Though Gideon had done his best to show his innocence, he had not succeeded. The jury found Gideon guilty of breaking into the pool hall and stealing beer, wine, and coins from two vending machines. McCrary delayed sentencing so he could review Gideon's prior record. It included a long list of petty crimes beginning in his youth.[7]

## A Man Adrift

Who was Clarence Earl Gideon? To his neighbors in Bay Harbor, Florida, he was known as a poor drifter. He moved about, working odd jobs and gambling, mostly running card games. He was born in Hannibal, Missouri, August 30, 1910. This made him fifty-one at the time of *State of Florida* v. *Gideon*. Anthony described Gideon in his book *Gideon's Trumpet*: "Gideon seems a man whose own private hopes and fears have long since been deadened by adversity—a used up man, looking fifteen years older than his actual age."[8]

According to a long letter about his life he would later write for one of his attorneys, his father died shortly after Gideon turned three years old. Gideon described his stepfather as a good, hardworking man. Gideon's upbringing was strict, and at the age of fourteen he ran away from home. His first run-in with the law was about a year later when he was caught stealing clothes; he had been living outdoors and the weather had turned cold. He was tried in the juvenile courts of Ralls County, Missouri, and sent to a reformatory for three years. After his release, he worked in a shoe factory, moving up to better-paying jobs. He got married, and the couple did well for about a year, until Gideon lost his job, committed some crimes, and was arrested. He had a court-appointed attorney for his trial. He was found guilty of larceny and burglary and—because he was eighteen years old by then—was sentenced to ten years in a Missouri prison. He received parole after three years.[9] It was 1932. The country was in the midst of the Great Depression, so jobs were scarce.

# Bumbling Through His Defense

Henry Fonda as Clarence Gideon speaks slowly and hesitantly, trying to think on his feet as he questions each witness. Judge McCrary (played by Richard McKenzie) gently guides Gideon through what he can and cannot do during cross-examination of witnesses. The movie shows how Gideon struggles to ask meaningful questions. He asks the eyewitness, named Lester Wade in the movie, how he knew the defendant was carrying a pint of wine. When he tries to cross-examine the pool hall owner, Leo Stafford, he asks him to describe the "bar part of the poolroom." Stafford appears confused, looking around as he says. "It's a long bar—down the middle of the room. It's just a bar."[10] Fonda looks at Stafford, turns, and heads back to his table without saying anything more. The judge dismisses the witness.

Though Gideon called several witnesses in his own defense, including the police officers who arrested him, in the movie his only witness is his former landlady, Edna Curtis (played by Fay Wray). She answers no to each of his questions: "Did you ever know me of being out drunk?" "Did you ever see me drunk?" "Did you ever hear of me getting drunk?"[11] Fonda portrays Gideon as satisfied with her answers, confident that this testimony proved he was not guilty of breaking into the poolroom with the intent to steal.

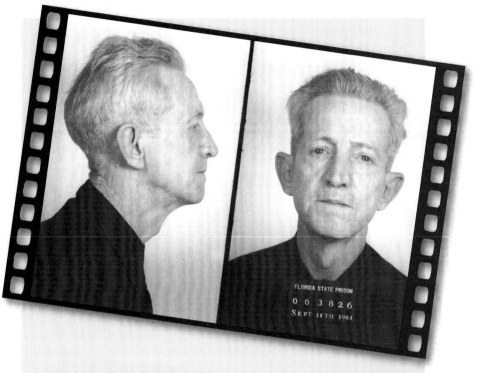

FLORIDA STATE PRISON
0 0 3 8 2 6
SEPT 11TH 1961

These mug shots taken after Gideon's arrest are in the Florida State Archives.

Gideon spent his young adulthood in and out of prison. This included a three-year sentence for a federal charge of possessing government property. He even escaped from a ten-year sentence in Missouri. He used forged documents to get a job with the railroad. Freedom was short-lived, however. *True Detective Magazine* included Gideon on its "wanted" list, and he was captured.[12]

By 1953, he had another marriage and another prison sentence behind him. He was now "doing time" of another sort; he was hospitalized with tuberculosis, an infectious lung disease. He eventually had surgery to remove a section of his right lung.

He married twice more, bought and sold a pool hall of his own, and had migrated to Florida by 1955. He married his fourth wife, Ruth Ada Babineaux. They remained married throughout the *Gideon* trials. Ruth had three children from a previous marriage, and she and Gideon had two sons and a daughter together. With such a large family, Gideon's absences, due to prison or tuberculosis, took a toll on her. She could not care for the children. They were placed in foster care, and Ruth began drinking heavily. Gideon left the hospital against his doctor's warning to reclaim his children. His ill health prevented him from holding a job. So he took to gambling.

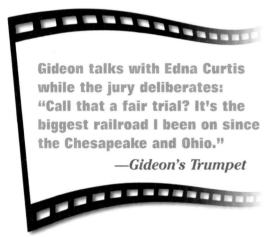

Gideon talks with Edna Curtis while the jury deliberates: "Call that a fair trial? It's the biggest railroad I been on since the Chesapeake and Ohio."

—*Gideon's Trumpet*

## The Sentence

Three days before Gideon's fifty-second birthday, on August 27, Judge McCrary handed down the maximum sentence of five years.[13] Gideon was on his way to a new home: Raiford Prison.

In a long letter Gideon wrote about his life, he described how he had been picked up and questioned, even arrested and held without charge, for various burglaries in Bay County in the months prior to the

June 3, 1961, charges.[14] Gideon felt at this point that his life was getting out of his control. He was losing both his health and his family, and he had struggled with the justice system—both criminal court and family court. Gideon fought back with a pencil and the law books at the final penitentiary to house him. And it made a difference.

# Chapter 3

# A Gambler Tries to Beat the Odds

Gideon worked at Raiford Prison, a minimum-security prison, as a mechanic. During his free time, he studied the law books from the library. This included a book of rules provided by the Supreme Court. He later admitted to a prison visitor that he didn't fully understand the books he read: "The rules take a pretty educated man to understand them," he said.[1] Still, he tried to follow them. These rules spell out what is necessary for the Supreme Court to consider a petition and grant a hearing for the case. If a hearing is granted, a *writ*, or official written order, is issued by the Supreme Court to a lower court. Known as a *writ of certiorari*, it requests that the original court's case files be sent for review by the upper court.

## Requesting Release

Gideon followed the examples of legal documents, writs, and other paperwork he found in the library books. He also followed the steps he found in the law books. He had help from Joe Peel, another inmate who had been an attorney and judge before entering prison. First, Gideon drafted a petition for a writ of habeas corpus. Literally, *habeas corpus* means "you should have the body." It is a petition used to request that a prisoner be released. This was sent to the Florida Supreme Court. Gideon did not ask for an appeal or reversal of the circuit court verdict. He simply challenged that verdict. In the book about Gideon's case, Anthony Lewis explained, "In Florida a prisoner may challenge the constitutionality of his conviction by petitioning the state supreme court to issue a writ of habeas corpus. Gideon had done just that, stating his constitutional claim for counsel again in the petition."[2] The Florida Supreme Court passed on that petition. They denied Gideon's claim.

This step in the process became the second case in the *Gideon* trials—*Gideon* v. *Cochran* (1961). The Florida Supreme Court's denial in granting the writ opened the way for Gideon to take the next step. He took his claim to a higher court—the Supreme Court of the United States.

## A Determined Inmate

Again following the examples in the law books, along with the list of rules provided by the U.S. Supreme Court,

The Supreme Court is the highest court in the United States. Article III of the U.S. Constitution provided for its creation. Nine members make up the Supreme Court—a chief justice and eight associate justices. The court's purpose is to interpret the Constitution's general legal rules in deciding on specific legal cases to determine the meaning and application in present terms.

This court is different from other courts, where several judges preside over trials on their individual dockets (or schedule) for that day. Instead of trials, the Court holds hearings in which debate takes place. Attorneys or representatives for each side argue their case, first in a written brief and then during oral arguments. During the oral arguments, the justices ask questions. They might also make comments on the logic or basis for the argument. After the oral arguments, the justices discuss the issue in private. They take a vote and then circulate memorandums on the case in which they offer their opinions. A justice might agree with the majority vote and his comments become part of the written majority opinion. He might disagree and write a dissenting opinion. Or he might agree but for different reasons than the others and write a concurring opinion to express his own view. These opinions become a written decision and are published in the *United States Reports*.

In 1962, when Gideon petitioned the Supreme Court, the chief justice was Earl Warren, so the Court was referred to as the Warren Court. The associate justices on this Court were Arthur J. Goldberg, Byron R. White, Potter Stewart, William J. Brennan, Jr., John Marshall Harlan, Tom C. Clark, William O. Douglas, and Hugo L. Black.

An inmate makes license plates at Raiford Prison.

Gideon began drafting a new petition. This included a notarized affidavit—a signed and witnessed statement—for submitting *in forma pauperis*. Literally, *in forma pauperis* means "in the manner of a pauper." A pauper is a very poor person. This type of submission means the petitioner has no money to cover court fees or costs. Normally, petitions required submitting forty printed copies, and the rules for formatting the document were very specific. Other items also had to be included, such as a copy of the lower court's opinion and a transcript. Providing these items is very expensive, so they were not required for *in forma pauperis* petitions, such as Gideon's.

He did not have access to a typewriter, so he used a pencil and stationery provided by the prison to carefully print his second petition. This time he was asking the highest court in the land to issue a writ of certiorari, or to agree to hear the case. Gideon did not actually ask the Supreme Court to dismiss his conviction. He wrote: "Petitioner asks this Honorable Court to consider the same arguments and authorities cited in the petition for Writ of Habeus [sic] Corpus before the Florida Supreme Court. In consideration of this petition for a Writ of Certiorari."[3]

## Gideon's Argument

In careful block printing on the lined paper printed with "Division of Corrections, Correspondence Regulations," Gideon presented his case. His argument centered on an unfair trial, having been denied due process of law under the Fourteenth Amendment. Despite misspellings and sometimes poor grammar and punctuation, he included legal terms and phrasing, such as "Comes now the petitioner," and "petitioner alleges"[4] to present his case. For two pages he explained events in his case, referring to "due process." It was not clear from the petition, though, how his original conviction violated "due process."[5]

Finally, the petition mentioned the key issue in Gideon's argument. "When at the time of the petitioners trial he ask the lower court for the aid of counsel, the court refused this aid. Petitioner told the court that this Court made decision to the effect that all citizens tried for a felony crime should have aid of counsel. The lower court ignored this plea."[6]

In the remaining pages of the petition, this denial of requested counsel is mentioned five more times. Clearly, Gideon saw the denial of an attorney when he could not afford one and had asked for one as ignoring his fundamental right under the Constitution. In his mind, this prevented him from receiving due process under the law. Anthony Lewis, who had interviewed Gideon, stated, "From the day he was tried Gideon had had one idea: That under the Constitution of the United States he, a poor man, was flatly entitled to have a lawyer provided to help in his defense."[7]

Gideon's petition stressed the Constitution and those rights that he believed it provided him as a U.S. citizen. He did not mention an important case presented to the U.S. Supreme Court twenty years earlier: *Betts* v. *Brady*. It had set a precedent. In other words, it created a framework for state courts to use in deciding when to provide counsel for poor defendants. The *Betts* v. *Brady*

# What Are the Right to Counsel Cases?

The Sixth Amendment says that people accused of crimes shall have the assistance of counsel for their defense. This was interpreted as having the right to hire a lawyer. It is now interpreted as having counsel appointed if one cannot be hired. As cases are brought before the Supreme Court for review, this basic right to counsel has expanded.

- *Powell* v. *Alabama* (1932). This applied to state cases. In death penalty cases, the state must provide counsel for poor people. This arose out of the case of the Scottsboro Boys, nine African Americans who were accused of raping two women. They were given little time to meet with their lawyers, and all but one were found guilty and sentenced to death. The Supreme Court overturned their convictions.

- *Johnson* v. *Zerbst* (1938). This applied to cases in federal court. Legal counsel was required for defendants too poor to hire a lawyer when charged with federal felonies.

- *Betts* v. *Brady* (1942). This applied to all noncapital crimes (crimes that would not incur a sentence of death or life in prison). The Supreme Court ruled that even a poor defendant could represent himself in noncapital cases unless special circumstances were present.

- *Gideon* v. *Wainwright* (1963). Even in noncapital cases, a defendant benefits from counsel. Poor defendants have the right to have an attorney provided for them.

- *Escobedo* v. *Illinois* (1964). The Court held that people have the right to have an attorney present during police questioning, not only at trial.

case provided the basis for the decision Judge McCrary had made in denying Gideon's request for an attorney.

## Impact of *Betts*

*Betts* v. *Brady* had many similar details to Gideon's case. Smith Betts was arrested for robbery in Maryland. During his arraignment—when the charge is formerly made against a suspect and he must enter a plea of guilty or not guilty—Betts asked for a lawyer. He stated he could not afford one and wanted counsel appointed for him. His request was denied. The judge pointed out that in that county, only those poor people charged with rape or murder were given attorneys. Betts pleaded not guilty and waived his right to a jury. (This means he gave up his right to have a jury, agreeing to have the judge make the decision in his case instead.) He conducted his own defense, choosing not to testify in his own defense. He was found guilty and sentenced to eight years in prison. Like Gideon, Betts followed the proper path to the Supreme Court, and the Court agreed to review his case.

The *Betts* petition argued that the due process clause in the Fourteenth Amendment guaranteed counsel in state criminal trials. The Supreme Court rejected that argument with a vote of 6–3. In previous cases, the Court had listed special circumstances that required providing a defendant with legal counsel. These included youth, mental defect, illiteracy, an extremely complex case, and other factors the judge might decide could prevent a fair trial. Betts did not fit any of these special circumstances. He had called and examined witnesses. He had even sought to establish his alibi during the

DIVISION OF CORRECTIONS
## CORRESPONDENCE REGULATIONS

MAIL WILL NOT BE DELIVERED WHICH DOES NOT CONFORM WITH THESE RULES

No. 1 -- Only 2 letters each week, not to exceed 2 sheets letter-size 8 1/2 x 11" and written on one side only, and if ruled paper, do not write between lines. Your complete name must be signed at the close of your letter. Clippings, stamps, letters from other people, stationery or cash must not be enclosed in your letters.

No. 2 -- All letters must be addressed in the complete prison name of the inmate. Cell number, where applicable, and prison number must be placed in lower left corner of envelope, with your complete name and address in the upper left corner.

No. 3 -- Do not send any packages without a Package Permit. Unauthorized packages will be destroyed.

No. 4 -- Letters must be written in English only.

No. 5 -- Books, magazines, pamphlets, and newspapers of reputable character will be delivered only if mailed direct from the publisher.

No. 6 -- Money must be sent in the form of Postal Money Orders only, in the inmate's complete prison name and prison number.

INSTITUTION _____  CELL NUMBER _____

NAME _____  NUMBER _____

In The Supreme Court of The United States
Washington D.C.

Clarence Earl Gideon    |    Petition for a writ
    Petitioner    |    of Certiorari Directed
   vs.    |    To The Supreme Court
H.G. Cochran, Jr, as    |    State of Florida.
Director, Divisions    |    No. 890   Misc.
of corrections State
of Florida    OCT. TERM 1961
   U.S. Supreme Court

To: The Honorable Earl Warren, Chief
    Justice of the United States
     Comes now The petitioner, Clarence
Earl Gideon, a citizen of The United States
of America, in proper person, and appearing
as his own counsel. Who petitions this
Honorable Court for a Writ of Certiorari
directed to The Supreme Court of The State
of Florida. To review the order and Judge-
ment of the court below denying The
petitioner a writ of Habeus Corpus.
     Petitioner submits That The Supreme
Court of The United States has The authority
and Jurisdiction to review The final Judge-
ment of The Supreme Court of The State
of Florida the highest court of The State
Under sec. 344 (B) Title 28 U.S.C.A. and
Because the "Due process clause" of the

**Gideon wrote his petition for a writ of certiorari in pencil on lined paper, asking the U.S. Supreme Court to review his case.**

alleged robbery. The justices determined that "a trial without the assistance of counsel was not fundamentally unfair."[8] The Court also expressed concern about the implications the decision might have. If they were to rule for Betts, it would mean that the appointment of counsel was a requirement even in state criminal cases. This could prove costly for the states. The Supreme Court opposed Betts's contention. Each state would continue interpreting the special circumstances for appointment of counsel on a case-by-case basis.

## Fundamental Rights

Both Betts and Gideon stressed their constitutional rights. These are the basic rights and privileges of each citizen of the United States. The Supreme Court's job is to interpret the Constitution to make sure new laws maintain those basic rights. While the Fourteenth Amendment provides for our due process under the law, both Betts and Gideon took that to mean their right to an attorney.

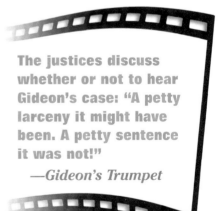

The justices discuss whether or not to hear Gideon's case: "A petty larceny it might have been. A petty sentence it was not!"

—*Gideon's Trumpet*

The justices focused on another point, however. The question they considered was: Is the right to counsel a fundamental right? Could someone accused of a crime have a fair trial without the help of a lawyer? A fair trial meant that due process was served. They felt Betts had received a fair trial. Gideon, however, felt the issue he raised was simple: He asked for a lawyer, and the court refused. Therefore his due process had been denied.

He may not have realized it, but he was really asking the Supreme Court to change its mind. In essence, he was asking them to overrule their own decision in *Betts* v. *Brady*.

## Against the Odds

Gideon was a gambler. Despite the odds, he thought he had a chance, and so he tossed his petition into the mix of thousands of others the Supreme Court receives annually. In 1962, the Court received roughly fifteen hundred *in forma pauperis* petitions each term. These are referred to as IFPs. About 90 percent of these cases were petitions for certiorari. Only about 13 percent of the regular petitions—and only 3 percent of the IFP petitions—made the Court's docket.[9] Gideon's petition arrived in the morning mail at the Supreme Court on January 8, 1962.

Gideon's IFP stirred activity and discussion within the offices of the Supreme Court. Clerks had been encouraged to keep a lookout for a case that was similar to *Betts*, since the Court had come close to overruling it earlier that term (which began October 1961). Gideon's petition showed promise. It was placed in a red envelope and held for thirty days. This allowed time for the state of Florida to submit a response or clarify background details. A copy of every IFP must be mailed by the petitioner to the respondent. When the state of Florida did not respond, a letter was sent to the attorney general of Florida asking for a response. By April, the Supreme Court had received a response, and

## Locating the Library

As soon as Gideon, played by Henry Fonda, settles into prison life, he finds the library. He walks in, seeing another inmate, Charley, sitting at a desk. Charley reads quietly while smoking his pipe. Charley looks up at Gideon who asks him, "You in charge here?" With pipe firmly between his teeth, Charley says, "That's right."

Gideon looks around. "I want to see everything you got on what rights a man has when he's on trial."

"Everything?" Charley asks. "You must be in for 200 years." He nods toward rows of books. "Right over there, second aisle."[10]

During most scenes to follow, Gideon is looking through a book. Whether he is in the dorm, in the yard, or watching others play basketball in the gym, Gideon is poring over a law book.

the IFP was circulated among the nine justices. When they met to discuss cases, this petition, *Gideon* v. *Cochran*, presented much debate. It was similar to *Betts* v. *Brady*, and it also called to mind the more recent *Carnley* v. *Cochran*.[11] The Court had come close to overturning *Betts* at that point. Was it now time to overturn it with Gideon?

# Chapter 4

# Before the Highest Court

Gideon's request had been granted. The justices agreed that it was time to reconsider the limits to providing counsel created by *Betts*. They decided they would review Gideon's case. The Court issued the formal order, or writ of certiorari, to the lower court—the Florida Supreme Court. Because Gideon's initial petition to the state challenged the decision of the Florida Division of Corrections, its director, H. G. Cochran, Jr., had been named in the suit. The Supreme Court would hold a hearing on the case named *Gideon* v. *Cochran*. This became the third case in the *Gideon* trials.

The questions the justices considered included: Are indigent defendants entitled to a lawyer, even in noncapital cases? Could a layman properly defend himself, as *Betts* v. *Brady* asserted? Or was it now time to overturn that ruling? Was Gideon afforded a fair trial?

## Preparing for a Supreme Court Hearing

Clarence Gideon and H. G. Cochran, Jr., were the litigants, or parties in the case. Abe Fortas, an attorney who would soon serve on the Supreme Court, was appointed to present Gideon's side. Bruce Jacob, assistant attorney general of Florida, would present Cochran's side in the claim against the state.

In a Supreme Court case, each attorney submits a written argument, called a brief, to the Court. They state their positions in the matter, citing prior case law, and try to persuade the justices to decide in their favor. The oral arguments, presented at the hearing, provide an opportunity for the justices to ask questions and clarify the position of each litigant.

In preparing for his brief, Jacob sent a letter to the attorneys general of all the other states. He felt it was important to let them know it was possible that *Betts* v. *Brady* might be overturned. Jacob later explained his reasoning: "My goal was to make sure the other states knew what was happening and what was at stake in *Gideon*, and that they were given an opportunity to become involved if they wished to do so."[1]

He asked them to consider submitting *amicus curiae* briefs. *Amicus curiae* literally means "friend of the court." An *amicus curiae* brief is a written response from a person or institution not personally involved in the

Earl Warren was chief justice of the Supreme Court from 1953 to 1969. During that time, the Court expanded constitutional protections.

lawsuit that supports a particular side of the case. The response was not what Jacob expected. Only about half the states responded, and those that did were not helpful to his side of the case.[2] Several states banded together to write a brief that was endorsed by twenty-three states and submitted as an *amicus curiae* brief on behalf of Gideon.[3]

The position of the state of Florida focused on the historical record showing that the Sixth Amendment "intended to ensure that defendants were free to retain their own counsel,"[4] that flexibility provided by the Fourteenth Amendment left the states to develop their own standards and systems, and that the special circumstances rule implied in *Betts* provided a "clear and workable standard."[5]

Jacob's brief also included a letter from Robert L. McCrary, Jr., stating: "Gideon had both the mental capacity and the experience in the courtroom at previous trials to adequately conduct his defense. . . . In my opinion he did as well as most lawyers could have done in handling the case."[6]

The brief concluded with the suggestion that overturning *Betts* would result in the release of more than half of Florida's prison inmates. According to the transcript of the oral argument, page 56 of Jacob's brief showed that 65 percent of Florida's prisoners did not have aid of counsel. The justice citing Jacob's brief estimated that about 5,200 prisoners would be affected by this decision.[7] Jacob recommended that a decision to overrule should not be retroactive—that is, it would not apply to people who had already been convicted without benefit of counsel, but only to cases from then on.[8] Such a ruling is called prospective. Since Gideon had brought the claim before the Court, he would be rewarded in a prospective ruling—the new rule would apply to him but not to old cases.

Author and political science professor John B. Taylor said that in the brief supporting Gideon, Abe Fortas "argued that a straightforward requirement of appointed counsel would be far less of an imposition on the states than continuing federal review of special circumstances, which would result in numerous reversals and retrials."[9] He suggested that the need for counsel is obvious and fundamental to a fair trial, stating: "Even a trained criminal lawyer will not undertake his own defense."[10] The introduction and several sections of the brief analyzed *Betts*, showing it unsatisfactory as a standard. A separate appendix analyzed Gideon's original case, showing how a trained lawyer would have benefitted the defendant.[11]

This brief was filed on November 21, 1962. As required, Fortas mailed a copy of the brief to Jacob, the opposing counsel, and sent one to Gideon.

## A Great Debate

On January 15, 1963, Abe Fortas stood at a lectern positioned between two tables. He stood before nine men dressed in black robes. In the center, sat Chief Justice Earl Warren. Fortas would speak first, since it was Gideon who had lost his case in the lower court. Then Bruce Jacob, arguing against Gideon and on behalf of the state of Florida, would speak. Both men would have approximately one hour each to make their cases.

Fortas is described as speaking forcefully but respectfully. In "his slow, southern-inflected baritone,"[12] he began with the customary greetings to the Court, then presented a summary of Gideon's first trial and his active participation and attempts to call and cross-examine witnesses. Upon this foundation, Fortas built his legal argument. He stressed the basic difficulties of *Betts* v. *Brady*: "It shows that no man, however intelligent, can conduct his own defense adequately."[13] He traced the history of right to counsel and the disadvantage of not having counsel; he discussed the case of the Scottsboro Boys (*Powell* v. *Alabama*) and concluded with *Betts*.

Fortas also outlined the research his staff had done. Thirty-seven states required counsel for poor defendants. Another eight provided counsel if requested. "That makes a total of 45 states that appoint counsel either by statute, court rule or by practice." That left five states that did so only in capital cases.[14] He pointed out the *amicus curiae* briefs provided by twenty-three states calling for the overturning of *Betts*.

He argued: "A criminal court is not properly constituted . . . under our adversary system of law unless there is a judge, and unless there is a counsel for the prosecution, and unless there is a counsel for the defense."[15] His concluding remarks urged the reversal of *Betts*.

A few justices asked questions during Fortas's address, including Justice Goldberg, who questioned the limits on supplying assistance of counsel. Other justices often added their own thoughts, considering how changes might shape the future of our legal system. They would then ask Fortas for input.[16]

## Fortas Argues for Gideon

In the movie, José Ferrer portrays Abe Fortas as a powerful speaker, impassioned, but respectful to both the Court and his fellow attorneys. In discussing a person's right to have adequate defense during a trial, he considers how he will make his case to the Court. "What I'd like to say to the Court is, Let's not talk; let's go down there and watch one of these fellows try to defend themselves."[17] In summing up his argument, he declares, "I think *Betts* v. *Brady* was wrong when it was decided. I think time has made that clear. And I think that the time has come that the correct rule, the civilized rule, the rule of individualism, the rule of due process must be stated by this Court."[18]

In reality, this is close to what Fortas said during his argument, but it was not his final statement. Though he did declare his belief that the Court had wrongly decided *Betts*, his final points referred the Court to parts of his written brief for their consideration while discussing the case.

Bruce R. Jacob, currently dean emeritus and professor of law at Stetson University College of Law, represented the state of Florida in *Gideon* v. *Wainwright*.

At 1:10 P.M., Bruce Jacob stood at the podium. He opened with a description of Gideon, including his age, race, and previous convictions. He objected to the inclusion of the transcript from *State of Florida* v. *Gideon*. This opening seemed to ruffle the feathers of Justice White. After that point, Jacob was bombarded with questions.[19] Jacob faced a different line of questions from those asked of Fortas. The justices often interrupted his presentation with queries: May I ask a question here? Is that true in your experience? Why do we have to waste time on that? How many have done this? What's your observation? About halfway into his argument, the justices asked Jacob to state his understanding of *Betts* and also *Powell*.[20]

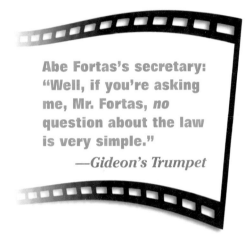

Abe Fortas's secretary: "Well, if you're asking me, Mr. Fortas, *no* question about the law is very simple."
—*Gideon's Trumpet*

Jacob stressed the consequences of overturning *Betts*, from the expense to taxpayers in states appointing counsel and the number of convicts—5,093 in Florida prisons—who were tried without counsel and might be released under new ruling.[21] He also "noted that states such as Florida had for 21 years followed 'in good faith' the 1942 Supreme Court ruling in the *Betts* case."[22]

Several times, Justice Potter Stewart commented that Gideon would not be allowed to represent another defendant in court. "Wouldn't Gideon maybe get in trouble for practicing law without a license?" Another justice added, "With the local bar association."[23] Jacob

Potter Stewart and the other justices questioned Bruce Jacob during
his oral argument for the state of Florida. Stewart noted that Gideon
would not be allowed to represent anyone else in court.

finally had to agree. He would later comment on how different he found the U.S. Supreme Court from the Florida Supreme Court. "Instead of asking about cases the way judges usually do—what did this case stand for, what did that case—they had all these hypothetical questions, trying to carry everything to its farthest point."[24]

At the conclusion of the hearing, Chief Justice Warren thanked the participants. The justices filed out of the courtroom. They would meet to discuss the issues presented and take a preliminary vote.

## Formulating the Decision

By the time the formal opinion on this case was issued, the case name had changed to *Gideon* v. *Wainwright*, since Cochran had stepped down as director of the Florida Division of Corrections. He was replaced by Louie L. Wainwright, who would now be the litigant in the case.

On the Friday following any oral arguments, the justices hold council. They meet to discuss the cases and then vote on each. If the chief justice is among the majority, he may either elect to write the case opinion or assign this duty to one of the other justices. If he is in the minority, the opinion is written by the senior justice (the member who has served longest on the Supreme Court) on the side of the majority. Following custom, the justices held a private vote on the appeal on Friday of the week they listened to the oral arguments in the *Gideon* case. Chief Justice Warren, who was in the majority, had the option of writing the opinion himself or passing the assignment on to an associate justice.

47

## Chosen for the Opinion

Justice Hugo Black had not agreed with his fellow justices in *Betts* v. *Brady*, and he wrote a dissent in that case. He protested that a layman could not adequately defend himself against a trained lawyer. He cited the Court's opinion in *Powell* v. *Alabama* that a defendant "requires the guiding hand of counsel in every step in the proceedings against him."[25] When Chief Justice Warren appointed Justice Black to write the opinion on the Court's decision in *Gideon* v. *Wainwright*, Black still had his original dissent from twenty years earlier. He used it as a framework and was able to circulate a draft within two weeks.[26]

This normally takes much longer. Careful thought must be given to the discussion of the Court, and the majority opinion must reflect that of the group. Other justices also need time to review and then write their personal opinions. Some might even change their votes after reflecting on cases and the majority view. The formal opinion on the decision of the Court was completed and announced on March 18, 1963, two months after the *Gideon* case was argued.

After the opinion is drafted, it circulates among the other justices who might add to the opinion, concurring or dissenting. During the circulation of the draft, justices occasionally change their vote. The final opinion reflects the final vote. The vote on *Gideon* v. *Wainwright* was unanimous.

Warren selected Justice Hugo Black to author the *Gideon* v. *Wainwright* decision. This was fitting. Black had served the longest of any justice on the Court—and he had delivered the dissent in *Betts*.

The ruling began: "The right of an indigent defendant in a criminal trial to have the assistance of counsel is a fundamental right essential to a fair trial, and petitioner's trial and conviction without the assistance of counsel violated the Fourteenth Amendment."[27]

Black mentioned the vast sums of money spent to prosecute defendants and that these prosecuting

## Where Was Gideon?

Gideon and Fortas never met each other. They communicated through letters. Though Gideon's complaint was argued before the Supreme Court, he was not present. He remained in prison. During the hearing taking place in Washington, D.C., Gideon stayed at Raiford Prison in Florida waiting for news. He received a letter telling him of the Court's decision. While he waited for a new trial, he remained at Raiford. Only when it was time to appear in circuit court was he transferred to the jail in Panama City.

Hugo Black was selected to write the opinion in the *Gideon* case. He was the longest serving justice on the Court and had written the dissent in the *Betts* case.

attorneys are "deemed essential to protect the public's interest in an orderly society. . . . That government hires lawyers to prosecute and defendants who have the money hire lawyers to defend are the strongest indications of the widespread belief that lawyers in criminal courts are necessities, not luxuries."[28]

In addition to condemning the *Betts* ruling, he summarized previous cases in the history of the right to counsel, including *Powell* v. *Alabama* and *Johnson* v. *Zerbst*, on which he had delivered the majority opinion. Justice Black wrote:

> We accept *Betts* v. *Brady*'s assumption, based as it was on our prior cases, that a provision of the Bill of Rights which is "fundamental and essential to a fair trial" is made obligatory upon the States by the Fourteenth Amendment. We think the Court in *Betts* was wrong, however, in concluding that the Sixth Amendment's guarantee of counsel is not one of these fundamental rights.[29]

The opinion concluded with the unanimous decision of the justices:

> The Court in *Betts* v. *Brady* departed from the sound wisdom upon which the Court's holding in *Powell* v. *Alabama* rested. Florida, supported by two other States, has asked that *Betts* v. *Brady* be left intact. Twenty-two States, as friends of the Court, argue that *Betts* was "an anachronism when handed down" and that it should now be overruled. We agree.[30]

Black's reasoning was disputed by Justice Harlan in a concurring opinion. He said that *Betts* had been consistent with *Powell*. However, Harlan said the time had come to overrule *Betts*.

# Chapter 5

# Not Over Yet: Gideon's New Trial

Gideon's story does not end with the Supreme Court ruling that he deserved a lawyer to represent him. Two questions still remained unanswered: Was Clarence Earl Gideon guilty or not guilty of the burglary at Bay Harbor Pool Room the night of June 3, 1961? And would a lawyer—the issue Gideon had so adamantly pursued—make a difference in his defense?

## Seeking Counsel

In late March, shortly after the Supreme Court ruling, Abe Fortas wrote to Gideon, suggesting a Florida lawyer represent him. Anthony Lewis, author of *Gideon's Trumpet,* describes correspondence from Fortas stating he had written to Tobias Simon, a lawyer from Miami who was associated with the Florida Civil Liberties Union, asking him to take Gideon's case.[1] Gideon wrote to Simon, who answered on April 15, 1963, assuring Gideon that a lawyer from the Florida Civil Liberties Union would indeed represent him.[2]

Though Gideon may have hoped he would be released, he would now stand trial again—this time with a lawyer. This did not sit well with Gideon, who complained in correspondence and during a meeting with his lawyer. He seemed convinced that to stand trial for the same crime was double jeopardy. He referred to the Fifth Amendment, which protected citizens from standing trial for the same crime at a later date. However, because Gideon had won the right to a new trial through his own action, this was not the case. Lewis summarizes this fact in his book: "A new trial won by a prisoner as a result of his own appeal is not double jeopardy under American law."[3]

During a meeting between Simon and Gideon, Simon reported to the ACLU that "Gideon spoke even more forcefully than in his letters"[4] about a second trial and became bitter at the thought of standing trial in the same courthouse in front of the same judge in Panama City, Florida, as before. He expressed doubt that he would receive a fair trial but finally agreed to allow Simon to represent him.

In early May, the Florida Supreme Court received the official mandate from the Supreme Court. It issued the order entitling Gideon to a new trial and the Circuit

Abe Fortas, who was later to become a Supreme Court justice, presented Gideon's case to the Court and helped with Gideon's appeal.

Court of Bay County, Florida, placed the case on the docket for July 5, 1963.

Irwin J. Block, an experienced criminal lawyer and former chief assistant prosecutor in Miami, had agreed to help Simon on Gideon's case. The men traveled to Panama City on July 4 to prepare for the case and meet with Gideon, who had arrived from Raiford Prison to the local jail. The meeting did not go well.

Lewis describes the events in *Gideon's Trumpet*, as reported by Tobias Simon and taken from court transcripts. Gideon refused to be represented and even refused to be tried. According to Simon, "he stated that

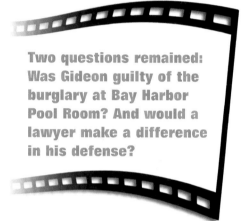

Two questions remained: Was Gideon guilty of the burglary at Bay Harbor Pool Room? And would a lawyer make a difference in his defense?

the court had no power to try him, and that his trial in Panama City would only mean his return to the penitentiary."[5] During the time scheduled for trial the next morning, Simon, Block, and Gideon met in the chambers of Judge Robert L. McCrary, Jr.

Gideon insisted on handling matters on his own, refusing to allow Block and Simon to act as his lawyers and expressing his wish to submit a motion to move his case to a different court so he could get a fair trial. Through questioning, Judge McCrary verified that Gideon did not want Simon or Block to represent him. The judge excused the lawyers but refused to allow Gideon to plead his own case again. A local lawyer, W. Fred Turner, was appointed to take the case and Gideon agreed, though he refused to allow the new public defender (appointed under Florida's public-defender law created in response to the Supreme Court ruling on *Gideon* v. *Wainwright*) to assist Turner.

## A New Lawyer

A new trial date of August 5, 1963, was set. Judge McCrary offered Gideon's release until that time on a one-thousand-dollar bond. Since Gideon could not raise bail, he was returned to Raiford Prison for another month.

While he awaited the new trial, his attorney, Turner, immediately set to work. He wrote to Judge McCrary on July 12 asking that the trial be postponed three weeks. He referred to the legal details and problems with the case "once considered so simple that the defendant could be required to try it himself on a few minutes' notice."[6] Since it was McCrary who had presumed it was a simple case back in 1961 (and reported it in response to the Supreme Court review), it is not surprising that McCrary denied Turner's request.[7] Turner also submitted a series of motions to change the location of the trial and dismiss the case. All were denied.

## The New Trial

At 9:00 A.M. on August 5, 1963, Gideon appeared in court once again, this time with Turner as his counsel, to face accusations that he had broken into and burglarized the Bay Harbor Pool Room on June 3, 1961. Turner was prepared, having spent three days talking with witnesses and investigating the allegations.

# Dramatic Defense

In the movie, Fred Turner (played by Lane Smith) is presented as very gracious and caring. He meets Gideon on the steps of the courthouse. He comments on Gideon's glasses and suit. They walk in together. As the trial begins, Turner is stately as he addresses the jury. When he questions or cross-examines witnesses, he is dramatic. He pauses, lowers or deepens his voice, and seems to punctuate important points.

When Turner questions Gideon, his actions have impact. He asks a series of questions, then heads toward his seat. He stops, turns, as if he has nearly forgotten something. "Oh, uh, one last thing," he says. "Mr. Stafford says you used to operate the poolroom for him on occasion. That right?" Gideon confirms. "How would you let yourself in for that purpose?" When Gideon states he had a key, Turner pauses. He slowly walks closer to Gideon. His next question is louder, forceful. "What do you say about these charges?"[8] While addressing the jury for closing arguments he is convincing, energizing, and captivating.

Anthony Lewis said Turner was "thin and dapper," reminding him of the dancer Fred Astaire.[9] Lane Smith conveys a man who seemed to dance before the court, choreographing his client's defense.

In the trial scene in the movie, Gideon is seated next to Fred Turner. Both lawyers set out their files as Judge McCrary begins.

JUDGE: What says the state? You ready?

HARRIS: Ready, your honor.

JUDGE: Defense ready?

TURNER: Ready, your honor [closes his briefcase].

GIDEON: Ready, your honor.

Turner stops, looks at Gideon, grins.[10]

The trial began with jury selection. Of twenty-eight men, six would sit on the jury. Turner questioned the first group of six men and dismissed two, providing no explanation to them or the court, something Gideon had not known he could do during the first trial. (These are called *peremptory challenges*; either side may dismiss a certain number of people from sitting on a jury without providing any reason.)

By 10:00 A.M., the jury for the trial had been sworn in. Assistant State Attorney William E. Harris, the original prosecutor on the case, made a two-minute opening statement. As he had stated at the first trial, the state intended to prove Gideon's guilt based on eyewitness testimony. Turner declined to make an opening statement for the defense.

The calling of witnesses was the next stage in the trial. Turner showed skill at cross-examination,[11] the questions asked after a witness's initial testimony. He also redirected, meaning that once the prosecutor finished cross-examining, Turner asked more questions to clarify a point. Again, this was something Gideon did not seem to know he could do in the first trial.

When a witness takes the stand, he answers questions to present facts or describe events to aid either the defense or the prosecution—whichever side has called the witness. Then the other side uses cross-examination to cast doubt on the testimony. Turner poked holes in the testimony of the chief witness for the prosecution, Henry Cook, eyewitness in the original trial.

During examination, or questioning, by the prosecutor, Cook stuck to his original story. Friends had dropped him off at the poolroom after attending a dance in

## Stuck on the Constitution

Despite all the work Gideon had done on his petitions, he did not understand the complexity surrounding his case. He cited cases such as *Kaiser* v. *State of Missouri*.[12] But he did not seem to understand the true legal issues. He clearly did not understand what his request meant. He wanted his case dismissed. It was not. But that is not what he asked of the Supreme Court. They did what he asked. They reviewed his case. And they made a decision in his favor.

But Gideon was stuck on his constitutional rights. In both petitions, he claimed his trial was unfair. He cited the Fourteenth Amendment's requirement for the due process of law. He cited the Sixth Amendment and his right to an attorney. Now that he faced a new trial, he cited the Fifth Amendment and claimed double jeopardy.

Gideon did not understand. Perhaps he did have help from someone who knew the law, as Bruce Jacob suggested. Despite his lack of understanding, though, he held a firm belief in our nation's Constitution. His lack of understanding and confusion of his legal rights demonstrated what Fortas had argued: A layman cannot adequately defend himself—especially not against a trained lawyer—even when the case is relatively simple.

Apalachicola, sixty miles away. He had seen Gideon inside the poolroom, saw him leave through a rear door, followed him down the alley to the telephone booth, and watched him drive off in a taxi. He stated that Gideon carried a bottle of wine, and his pockets were bulging (presumably with coins from the vandalized vending machines).

## A Skilled Defender

During cross-examination, Turner questioned why Cook's friends would have dropped him off at the poolroom rather than take him home. His home was only a few more blocks away, and they'd already driven sixty miles. Turner also got Cook to admit that advertisements covered the windows of the poolroom, which were high up on the building. He then asked Cook how he was able to see Gideon inside the poolroom with the windows situated as they were. Finally, he asked if Cook had ever been convicted of a felony—a line of questioning Gideon had attempted while pleading his own defense.

Cook admitted to having been on probation for stealing a car. Turner jumped on the discrepancy between this response and his denial of criminal history in the first trial. The two lawyers argued about this point and its importance in this trial. Finally, Judge McCrary allowed Turner to conclude cross-examination by asking whether Cook had ever denied being convicted of a felony and, if so, where and when that had taken place. The answer suggested he was guilty of lying about his criminal record in the previous trial. In fact, he had not lied, because he had been a juvenile at the time of the earlier incident, and juvenile delinquency was not a felony. Cook simply claimed he had been confused over terms. But his credibility was weakened.

As the trial progressed, Turner drew out new details in old testimony, including the fact that Ira Strickland, Jr., who had operated the poolroom at the time of the burglary, often asked Gideon to do odd jobs around the pool hall and that Gideon had on occasion run it for Strickland.[13] Actually, Gideon had a key to the pool hall at the time of the crime and would not have needed to break a window to enter the building.

Turner clarified the details of the burglary with Duell Pitts, the detective on the case. When Pitts had arrested Gideon, he said, he found that Gideon was carrying "twenty-five dollars and twenty-eight cents in quarters, nickels, dimes and a few pennies."[14] He carried no bills or paper money.

During the first trial, the taxi driver, Preston Bray, provided testimony that seemed to reflect Gideon's guilt. He quoted Gideon as saying, "Don't tell anyone you picked me up."[15] Turner got Bray to admit that whenever he picked up Gideon, the man made such a statement, apparently because he did not want his wife to know. According to Anthony Lewis, who attended the trial, he also verified that he had driven Gideon to the card game he had run that night— *before* Gideon acquired the winnings that would have made his pockets bulge with the weight of coins.[16] (However, attorney Bruce Jacob recalled the gambling taking place several days earlier.[17])

Finally, Turner presented a surprise witness, some-one who had not been called to testify during the first

The Supreme Court justices who decided the *Gideon* case were known as the "Warren Court," for Chief Justice Earl Warren, center.

trial. J. D. Henderson owned the grocery store in Bay Harbor. He testified that on the morning of June 3, 1961, Cook had admitted to him that he had been picked up for questioning regarding the poolroom break-in. Cook told Henderson that he thought the person he had seen might have been Gideon, but he was not certain. This contradicted Cook's testimony at both trials, in which he had indicated he was very certain that it *was* Gideon.[18] Cross-examination by the prosecutor served only to further lessen Cook's credibility.

Gideon was the final witness called. Questioning by his attorney was brief. Cross-examination by the prosecutor, Harris, centered around Gideon's lack of employment, the odd jobs he did, such as painting at the Bay Harbor Hotel in exchange for a free room, and the gambling he used to support himself.

By 2:40 P.M., the testimony had concluded. After a recess, the lawyers presented closing arguments. Turner's focused on the testimony of the key eyewitness, Henry Cook. He reiterated the facts that arose during his cross-examination: Cook supposedly saw Gideon commit this crime. He had told Irene Rhodes that the police should be called, but either he did not call the police or the police arrived before he could phone them. Turner suggested that Cook did indeed see Gideon that night from the alley, watched him use the pay phone, and that the beer and wine that had been stolen were never found because Cook was the lookout for his friends as *they* broke into the poolroom. Seeing Gideon provided a perfect cover-up for their crime, Turner said.

Assistant Prosecutor J. Paul Griffith made the closing remarks for the state, and he reiterated the facts as originally presented. Harris, the prosecutor, also added a rebuttal, or legal argument contradicting Turner's closing remarks. In the rebuttal, Harris emphasized his disbelief of Gideon's explanation that he was carrying around so much change because of his gambling activities.

## The Verdict

The jury entered deliberations at 4:20 P.M. An hour and five minutes later they returned with the verdict:

## Was Gideon Innocent?

Throughout his ordeal, Gideon declared his innocence. Turner presented facts that cast doubt on Gideon's guilt, such as having had a key to the pool hall. But others, including Bruce Jacob, felt he was guilty. The jury for the first trial found him guilty. According to Jacob, Gideon admitted during a presentence report to having taken coins and items from the pool hall. But he insisted he had not broken in.[19]

For a court to find the accused guilty, facts must prove that guilt. Any doubt suggests the accused may not be guilty as charged. This does not mean he has done no wrong. Turner cast enough doubt on the facts presented for the jury to find Gideon not guilty.

The issue before the Supreme Court was not an issue of innocence. It was whether or not Gideon had received a fair trial. They determined that a lawyer would help his case. Turner proved them right.

not guilty. Clarence Earl Gideon was now acquitted of a crime for which he had already served two years of a five-year sentence.

Anthony Lewis describes Gideon's reaction to the verdict: "After nearly two years in the state penitentiary Gideon was a free man. There were tears in his eyes, and he trembled even more than usual as he stood in a circle of well-wishers and discussed his plans."[20] Before being sent to prison, Gideon had arranged for his half brother to adopt his children. Gideon and his wife were separated, and he wanted to make sure they would be taken care of and would stay out of the foster-care system. He would see them once more before heading to Tallahassee to stay with a friend and move forward with his life.

That night he stopped in at the pool hall he had been accused of burglarizing. It was a triumphant visit. His steadfast belief in the rights of the poor and the protection of the Constitution helped equalize the justice system. The poor no longer had to fear being convicted despite their innocence. Public defenders would be provided and changes to the American criminal justice system had already begun.

# Chapter 6

# Watching History Unfold

*Gideon's Trumpet* is the 1980 Hallmark Hall of Fame television movie based on the book with the same title written by Anthony Lewis. Lewis, a journalist who covered the Supreme Court's decision in this case, wrote a book about Gideon's experience. It was published in 1964, shortly after Gideon's new trial. The movie, made sixteen years later, recaps the events leading up to the Supreme Court's decision in the landmark case *Gideon* v. *Wainwright*.

Henry Fonda portrays the semiliterate drifter, Clarence Earl Gideon. He presents a determined man, stubbornly pursuing his legal rights. He is finally

*Gideon's Trumpet*, the movie based on the *Gideon* case, opens with Henry Fonda, as Clarence Earl Gideon, making a statement about the events leading to his time in prison.

acquitted. His experience helps launch a major change to the U.S. criminal justice system.

The movie has been criticized for its unrealistic portrayal of prison and its pacing. The dorm, or barracks, style of housing and more fencing than bars led some critics to say it seemed more like a work farm or detention center than a prison. Despite the slow pace of the early court scenes,[1] the events are accurate and convey the sequence of Gideon's experiences. In addition to Henry Fonda, the cast includes notable actors John Houseman (as Chief Justice Earl Warren), José Ferrer (as Abe Fortas), Lane Smith (as Fred Turner), and Fay Wray (as Mrs. Curtis).

## Dawn of the Crime

The movie opens with Fonda as Raiford County prisoner #003826 making a statement about his life and the events leading to his incarceration. This is actually a short section of a longer scene that will be repeated toward the end of the movie. It is Gideon's response to a request from Abe Fortas asking for some personal information to help his staff in preparing a brief for the Supreme Court.

The movie flashes back to the night of the crime, June 3, 1961, when a deputy on nightly patrol stops outside Bay Harbor Pool Room. The door is ajar and a window broken. He uses the cruiser's radio, saying, "Mel, break-in at the poolroom. Y'better meet me."[2] He cautiously investigates. When he shines his flashlight into the entrance, the shaft of light reveals vending machines pried open. He questions a man standing at the corner of the building, near a pay phone.

## The TV Movie

Anthony Lewis, author of the book *Gideon's Trumpet*, cowrote the teleplay with producer David W. Rintels. The movie was released as a television movie airing as a Hallmark Hall of Fame special presentation on April 30, 1980. It was nominated for three Emmy Awards and featured a notable cast. Actress Fay Wray (who played King Kong's love interest decades earlier) made her final screen appearance in this movie, playing Mrs. Curtis. Anthony Lewis even made a cameo appearance—as the reporter at the end of the movie who asks Gideon about the outcome of the trial.

This witness claims he had just been dropped off at the pool hall after attending a dance. He says he saw Clarence Gideon exit the building with a pint of wine, make a phone call, and wait for his taxi. The deputy calls the owner, and when he arrives, he confirms that some beer, wine, Cokes, and cigarettes are missing, along with about five dollars from the cigarette machine and six dollars from the jukebox.

Police hunt for Gideon, locating him at a nearby bar, where he is having a drink. He is questioned and asked to empty his pockets. They are full of coins, mostly nickels, dimes, and quarters. Though he insists the money is his winnings from a card game, he is taken into custody.

Fonda portrays Gideon as a bit gruff and cantankerous, slow to speak and move, and hardheaded. At trial, he has no choice but to act as his own attorney. His attempts to call and question witnesses show his ineptitude at understanding and following court protocol. When the prosecutor objects to a question asked of the witness during cross-examination, the judge tells Gideon he can't ask such a question. His response is, "What can I ask?"[3]

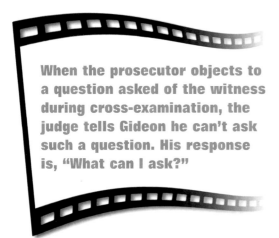

When the prosecutor objects to a question asked of the witness during cross-examination, the judge tells Gideon he can't ask such a question. His response is, "What can I ask?"

Fonda shows Gideon calmly but uncertainly doing his best to act the part of a lawyer, convinced that he is proving his innocence. Gideon asks the owner of Bay Harbor Pool Room to describe the interior of the pool hall. He concludes his defense by calling his former landlady. In the movie this is the only witness he calls, and he questions her about his drinking and use of the public telephone outside the pool hall.

## Condensing the Story

Though the order of events is quite accurate, several details are very different in the movie. Several names have been changed. Henry Cook, the key witness in the original trial, is a soft-spoken young man named Lester Wade. In the movie, the owner of the pool hall is Leo Stafford. The real owner was Ira Strickland. In addition, Edna Curtis, played by Fay Wray, seems to represent all the women in the story. In the movie, Mrs. Curtis is Gideon's landlady. In reality, Mrs. Morris was the

Veteran actors portrayed a number of roles in *Gideon's Trumpet:*
Lane Smith (top) was Fred Turner; John Houseman played Earl
Warren; and in her last screen role, Fay Wray played Mrs. Curtis.

71

## Gideon Researches His Rights

Gideon arrives at Raiford Prison, prisoner #003826. He quickly locates the library and, looking around, asks the inmate sitting at a desk, how to find "what rights a man's got during trial."[4] The library worker points to the rows upon rows of law books. He explains to Gideon that there are steps in an appeal process and he must do three things: file a writ of habeas corpus, file a writ of certiorari, and provide an affidavit of application *in forma pauperis*.

The movie shows Gideon in different prison scenes, mostly during free time—in the barracks, in the yard, in the gym. He studies the books and works on his petition. He becomes known for what he is doing, and other inmates want to share their stories of innocence with him.

Like the role Henry Fonda plays, the real Gideon took advantage of the library at Raiford, and as he studied, he came to realize there were many prisoners in jail due to circumstances similar to his own.

landlady, and her neighbor Irene Rhodes testified at the first trial about seeing Gideon make the phone call.

Some events seem to happen too quickly. For instance, Judge McCrary requested information on Gideon's past record before deciding his sentence. In the movie, sentencing occurs immediately after the verdict. While the jury is out, Gideon and Mrs. Curtis talk. Gideon worries that he might be found guilty and could get "six months. A year even."[5] The viewer is shocked to hear that Gideon receives the maximum sentence—five years.

## Plenty of Free Time

Though the first court scene seems slow-paced compared to the action of today's movies, the movie picks up speed as Gideon arrives at Raiford Prison. When he is not working as a mechanic, Fonda's character locates the library and spends free time reading the law books that take up most of the shelving. The other inmates are aware of Gideon's studying and his intent to petition the Florida Supreme Court and the U.S. Supreme Court. They share their personal stories and ask for Gideon's advice. Gideon talks about his case and the laws he is reading with the library inmate, Charley. Charley shakes his head. "Couple months in this place and they all think you are Moses, come to lead them to the promised land. Well, maybe you are."[6]

When Gideon mails the petition, a crowd of inmates follows him, growing in number as he reaches the post office. One guy asks to hold the letter. When Gideon takes it back, Fonda portrays him as forcefully stuffing it into the mail slot. These scenes showing the men loitering or seemingly on free time led to critics of the movie stating that the prison seemed to be "a sort of summer camp for adult males."[7]

The scenes of activity and discussion within the Supreme Court are the most engaging in this movie. They show the process such petitions undergo, from the clerks opening the mail to discussion of Gideon's petition and the memorandum for the review board. The justices discuss the need for an absolute rule on the right to counsel and the necessity of overturning *Betts* v. *Brady*.

When the response arrives from the Supreme Court, the news spreads, and Fonda's character is located at his mechanic's job. His walk to pick up these letters is again shown with a crowd of other inmates following him to the post office. The yard is full of prisoners, dressed in prison garb of blue jeans and chambray shirts, eager to hear what the letters say. "It means they agreed to hear it, still got to win it," Gideon says.[8]

Abe Fortas, played by José Ferrer, is appointed by the Supreme Court to argue the case. The scenes in which his staff discusses Gideon's background and prior offenses, the arguments to present, and questions to investigate in preparing the case are also very engaging. They provide an overview of the lawyers' thought processes. For example, they researched how state law on the appointment of counsel had changed over the years, compiling numbers on the present interpretation of each state. How many previous verdicts might be reversed if the Court ruled in Gideon's favor? What impact should the law have? How would it work and shape our futures?

Fonda, as Gideon, holds the letter containing his petition to the Supreme Court.

## Before the Supreme Court

José Ferrer portrays Abe Fortas as an attorney intrigued by the questions the case raises and the potential impact it can have on the future workings of the criminal justice system. Despite these details, he pledges that his highest priority will be helping the accused by getting Gideon out of prison. This section of the movie is filled with facts and details about the cases that had come before the *Gideon* case.

During oral arguments before the Supreme Court, Ferrer portrays an impassioned Fortas who stresses that the Gideon matter illustrates the fact that a defendant cannot have a fair trial without counsel and that counsel should be provided at least from the point of arraignment. Fortas states, "The law must be stable yet not stand still."[9] The justices agree unanimously to overturn the *Betts* ruling.

## Adding Clarity

In a few scenes, the movie clarifies points from the actual events. During opening arguments in the first trial, the prosecutor explains to the jury that a small sum of money was taken, making the crime a petty larceny. That would make it a misdemeanor. The charge of breaking and entering made it a felony.

Also, throughout scenes surrounding the Supreme Court, details about the process are shared aloud so the viewer understands what is happening. Both the group of justices and Fortas's staff ask questions to show the impact the ruling could have.

Finally, the Court actually broke for lunch in the middle of Fortas's oral argument, and he continued

The renowned actor José Ferrer played Abe Fortas, the attorney who argued *Gideon* in front of the Supreme Court.

after lunch. Also, both sides had another speaker to address the Court. In the movie, only Fortas and Jacob speak before a courtroom full of spectators. According to Jacob, other than the justices and attorneys, only his wife and Anthony Lewis were in the courtroom.[10]

In the movie, while the justices allow Fortas to basically make a speech, with a few questions asked and little debate, in reality, Fortas responded to many questions raised by the justices. The movie emphasizes the contrast between the two attorneys when Jacob takes the podium. The justices fire questions at him. They interrupt. His voice shakes just slightly. This scene focuses on the number of inmates Jacob is concerned may be released. The scene concludes with Chief Justice Warren getting Jacob to admit that some of the roughly five thousand inmates tried with a lawyer were illiterate. His voice is strict as he declares, "Any illiterate among those five thousand has been deprived of his constitutional rights!"[11] Jacob looks chastised, closes his notebook, and returns to his seat.

## A Few Flaws

The movie does have some flaws. First, the chronology of the events of the final trial and Gideon's release from prison are confusing. The movie shows the whole prison cheering for Gideon when he is released and walks out the front doors of Raiford Prison; in reality, he had to stay in prison because he could not come up with bail. The change in defense lawyers (in which Tobias Simon and Irwin Block were replaced with Fred Turner) blends together. In reality, Gideon's refusal to have these men

# What About the Real Characters?

The movie *Gideon's Trumpet* shows real people, both famous and little-known. What happened to them after the *Gideon* trials?

Abe Fortas continued to be a defender of civil liberties. In 1965, President Lyndon B. Johnson appointed him as an associate justice of the Supreme Court. Three years later, President Johnson nominated him to replace retiring Chief Justice Earl Warren. But the Senate discovered that Fortas had accepted lecture fees, an activity considered improper. They debated his appointment. So Fortas asked President Johnson to withdraw the nomination. He served another year on the Supreme Court before resigning in 1969. He returned to his law practice. Fortas died in 1981.

Bruce Jacob built a distinguished career in law. He had already moved into private practice at the time of *Gideon*. He eventually became a professor at Emory School of Law, where he helped set up a Legal Assistance for Inmates Program at Atlanta Penitentiary. He eventually returned to Florida to teach at one of his alma maters, Stetson University College of Law. He is currently dean emeritus and continues to teach criminal and constitutional law.

Very little is known about Clarence Gideon's life after the trials. He continued to drift around and married once more. In the words of crime historian David Krajicek, Gideon "resumed his place in a well-worn rut."[12] He is said to have been very proud of *Gideon's Trumpet* by Anthony Lewis. One story went around that he was once arrested for loitering. But he showed a copy of the book and was released.[13] He died in Fort Lauderdale, Florida, on January 18, 1972, at the age of sixty-one.

defend him took place in the judge's office. In the movie, the men approach the bench and it takes place there.

In any case, Fred Turner (Lane Smith) engages the viewer with his cross-examination, which trips up the chief witness and widens the holes in the prosecution's case. As was apparent in the first trial scene in which Gideon fumbled in defending himself, the viewer is led to believe that Gideon is not guilty. So the verdict "not guilty" is a satisfying conclusion. Not only is this the case, but throughout the movie, few doubts exist that Gideon was anything but innocent. The viewer is convinced. The movie stresses how this down-and-out man who has had his share of run-ins with the law was unjustly accused.

The movie wraps up with the quote by Robert Kennedy. It is read as voice-over by John Houseman, who also played Chief Justice Earl Warren. The viewer listens as Gideon walks down the street. The statement, from November 1, 1963, applauds the strong belief of one man to do something to change what he viewed as an injustice.

# Chapter 7

# The Promise of Gideon

A poor man's reaction to what he considered unjust treatment had tremendous impact on the U.S. legal system. The Supreme Court ruling in *Gideon* v. *Wainwright* helped equalize the justice system for the poor and ensure against conviction of the innocent. It has brought about some of the biggest changes in the history of American criminal justice.

Before Gideon's new trial was scheduled, states sprang into action to deal with the Supreme Court's new ruling. Overturning *Betts* and declaring that indigent defendants were entitled to an attorney in all criminal cases meant provisions had to be made. Not only were funds needed to pay the lawyers who would be assigned these cases, a pool of lawyers was needed to draw upon.

Bruce Jacob's prediction that overturning *Betts* would burden the states did not come true. Thirty-seven states were already guaranteeing counsel in all felony cases, and eight others were doing so at least in the larger cities. Twenty-four were doing so in both felony and misdemeanor cases. Only five southern states—Florida, Alabama, North Carolina, South Carolina, and Mississippi—were seriously affected due to their provision for counsel only in capital cases.[1] While these states worked to address the Court's new ruling, other states upgraded the steps they already had in place. Most found the changes beneficial. According to John B. Taylor, author and political science professor: "Disputes over the need for counsel were eliminated; convictions of the truly guilty were less vulnerable to being overturned; the burden on appellate courts was reduced; and most fundamentally, hapless defendants were no longer required to fend for themselves."[2]

## Florida's Response

Shortly after the Supreme Court ruling, Florida governor Farris Bryant asked the legislature to enact a public defense system in the state. Within two months, May 1963, it was approved. The statute required "a public defender in each of the state's sixteen judicial circuits."[3]

In the *Gideon* decision, the Supreme Court had left some questions unanswered. Among them was whether to make the decision retroactive. This would

## Gideon's Legacy

On November 1, 1963, Attorney General Robert Kennedy spoke to the New England Law Institute about the impact of *Gideon* v. *Wainwright*. He said:

> If an obscure Florida convict named Clarence Earl Gideon had not sat down in prison with a pencil and paper to write a letter to the Supreme Court, and if the Supreme Court had not taken the trouble to look for merit in that one crude petition among all the bundles of mail it must receive every day, the vast machinery of American law would have gone on functioning undisturbed.
>
> But Gideon did write that letter. The Court did look into his case and he was retried with the help of a competent defense counsel, found not guilty, and released from prison after two years of punishment for a crime he did not commit, and the whole course of American legal history has been changed.[4]

mean that the Division of Corrections would have to go back and look at all the prisoners who did not have counsel appointed at their trials. They might need to be released. If the decision were not retroactive, those prisoners would remain incarcerated, but the ruling would apply to all future trials.

In the fall of 1963, a group of ten Florida prisoners asked the Supreme Court to rule on this unanswered question. The Court simply overturned their convictions and sent the cases back to the Florida Supreme Court to review "for further consideration in light of *Gideon* v. *Wainwright*."[5] By January 1964, 976 prisoners had been released and another 500 were back in court for new trials.[6] Petitions from others continued arriving for review. (In 1967, in the case *Burget* v. *Texas*, the Supreme Court applied *Gideon* retroactively.)

The *Gideon* ruling also left the question of how far-reaching counsel for the poor should go. It does not extend to civil cases. Civil court would handle damages due to accident, fines for being accused of breaking local codes, eviction, and child abuse charges. Isn't what these poor might lose equal to loss of life or liberty? So far the Supreme Court has not seen it this way.

## The Public Defense System

Another shake-up taking place in the judicial system was the issue of what kinds of lawyers should be provided for indigent defendants and how they should be compensated. In states making provision for legal counsel, the lawyers appointed by judges were often not paid or were new and inexperienced lawyers. In 1961, Attorney General Robert F. Kennedy had appointed a committee to review provisions for the indigent in federal courts. Made up of scholars, state and federal judges, and practicing lawyers, they came up with four possible methods for creating a pool to draw from when appointing counsel to the indigent cases in federal court. Their recommendations were submitted to Congress as the Criminal Justice Act of 1963. This took place just ten days before the *Gideon* decision was announced.[7] So *Gideon* encouraged action on this issue.

The issue at the state level was more difficult, because there are many more state than federal trials. The solution seemed to lie in how law students were trained. Experts in criminal law cited the need for elevating criminal law, providing more exposure during school, providing trial experience, and incorporating social responsibility among corporate lawyers.[8] In addition, an office for public defenders or voluntary legal aid seemed necessary, according to Whitney Seymour, who in 1963 headed the American Bar Association's task force on counsel for the indigent.[9] New York's Legal Aid Society provided counsel for sixty thousand criminal cases a year.[10] Both Connecticut[11] and California had had Offices of the Public Defender since the early 1900s, and at the time of *Gideon*, a total of thirteen states had them at least in their largest cities.[12] Necessary changes were now fueled by the Supreme Court's latest ruling.

*Robert F. Kennedy said:*
**"Gideon did write that letter . . . and the whole course of American legal history has been changed."**

Clarence Earl Gideon died in 1972 and was buried in an unmarked grave. The American Civil Liberties Union donated a tombstone in honor of Gideon's fight for constitutional rights.

In a letter celebrating the fortieth anniversary of the Court's decision, U.S. senator Joseph I. Lieberman (D.-Conn.) wrote that *Gideon* did more than guarantee counsel for the poor: "The case was a turning point in our legal system. . . . It established the role of the public defender in providing an advocate for those who do not have the resources to afford a lawyer."[13]

## The Promise and the Problems

Today's public defense system fulfills one of the promises of the *Gideon* decision. Various methods are used to appoint attorneys. Rita Fry, public defender in Cook County, Illinois, wrote: "Today, states and localities aim to fulfill these obligations through state or local public defender organizations, appointed counsel, or through a contracting process."[14] Eighty percent of defendants in criminal cases receive aid for legal counsel.[15] Connecticut and Kentucky are leaders among the states for strong public defense. But in other states, public defenders struggle to keep from getting buried in large numbers of cases.

## Is Everyone Entitled to a Lawyer?

Many questions were left unanswered by the Supreme Court's ruling in *Gideon* v. *Wainwright* in 1963. Most have been answered in the years since. Subsequent rulings have expanded that 1963 ruling. In 1972, the year Gideon died, the Supreme Court expanded its ruling on free counsel yet again. According to David Krajicek, "Anyone arrested who might spend even one day in jail if convicted, including those charged with misdemeanor crimes," has the right to free counsel.[16] But this still does not include every instance when the poor are forced to appear in court. Who will pay court costs or pay a lawyer when the poor find themselves the victim of crimes? Our justice system is living. It changes, expands, evolves. And needed changes can still take place. Gideon proved that even a poor, uneducated person can bring about such changes.

This is especially crucial, because another promise of *Gideon* is right to counsel early in the criminal justice process. When more defendants exist than defenders able to assist them, what happens? Do they receive counsel during arraignment or only hours before they appear for their trial?

The number of defendants continually exceeds the number of available defenders. This creates problems in funding as well as overworked attorneys who cannot adequately prepare or are only able to meet with a defendant shortly before a trial. In many states, such as Massachusetts, conditions are worsening. Funds are lacking, and defendants sometimes sit in jail for several weeks or months awaiting representation. This was the case, as reported by journalist Joshua Krumholz, when the problem reached crisis level in Massachusetts. "Money paid to private attorneys retained by the state to represent indigents was so low, that attorneys stopped handling cases by the hundreds."[17] The Massachusetts legislature implemented a reform of the system in 2005.

According to a report by Senator Edward Kennedy, more states are investigating their public defense for the poor. Problems remain. Pennsylvania reports lack of funding for county public defender offices. Kennedy wrote: "A Georgia Supreme Court commission described that state's system as inadequate, unconstitutional, and responsible for much needless incarceration."[18]

Reports from many states include terrible situations in which poor defendants wait in county jails for months or years before they see a lawyer or meet with their appointed lawyer for a brief time just before trial.

Some of these are noncapital offenses and even misdemeanor and juvenile cases.

Kennedy calls for reform in all sectors of our justice system:

> All states should provide adequate resources for indigent defense by funding public defender offices and paying fair rates for lawyers appointed to represent indigent defendants. We should no more tolerate a difference in justice between federal courts and state courts than a difference in justice between defendants who can afford counsel and those who cannot.[19]

When an attorney is handling sixteen hundred misdemeanor cases per year in addition to his private caseload, he has little time to be an effective advocate for his clients. According to commentary by Leonardo Castro in *Minnesota Lawyer*: "If the public is expected to respect our court system, and lawyers and judges are expected to enhance the trust and confidence of our justice system, we must learn to distinguish between the administration of courts and the administration of justice."[20] He explains that justice is a process that requires both time and resources for each step.

Today, the right to counsel is taken for granted. It is not in question. Joshua Krumholz states, "It is a critical cog in the machine that protects our citizens from government over-reaching and intrusion."[21] A poor, semiliterate man believed it should be something all Americans could assume as their right and persisted in making it so. Perhaps in the future, the adequate funding and resources to keep the public defense system running smoothly will be something this country can count on, too.

**Confronting the Court**

1. David Krajicek, "A Florida Burglary, review of the case on Court TV," *Court TV Crime Library*, chapter 1, n.d., <http://www.crimelibrary.com/gangsters_outlaws/cops_others/ clarence_gideon> (May 4, 2007).

2. Leonardo Castro, "'Gideon' turns 40: a look at the case, and its future," *Minnesota Lawyer*, March 24, 2003, p. 1; and Anthony Lewis, *Gideon's Trumpet* (New York: Random House, 1964, 1980), p. 10.

3. "Case Background," *Gideon at 40: Understanding the Right to Counsel*, p. 2, National Association of Criminal Defense Lawyers Web site, n.d., <http://www.nacdl.org/ gideon> (November 12, 2006).

4. "The Story of *Gideon* v. *Wainwright*," State of Connecticut Division of Public Defender Services Web site, n.d., <http://www.ocpd.state.ct.us/Content/Gideon/Gideon% 20Story.htm> (November 12, 2006).

5. "The Bill of Rights," The National Constitution Center Web site, © 2008, <http://www.constitutioncenter.org/explore/ TheU.S.Constitution/index.shtml> (April 27, 2007).

6. James J. Tomkovicz, *The Right to the Assistance of Counsel* (Westport, Conn.: Greenwood Press, 2002), pp. 18–20.

7. Lewis, p. 138.

8. Tomkovicz, p. 30.

9. Lewis, p. 115.

**Alone and on Trial**

1. "Case Background," *Gideon at 40: Understanding the Right to Counsel*, p. 2, National Association of Criminal Defense Lawyers Web site, n.d., <http://www.nacdl.org/gideon> (November 12, 2006).

2. Anthony Lewis, *Gideon's Trumpet* (New York: Random House, 1964, 1980), p. 64.

3. David Krajicek, "A Florida Burglary, review of the case on Court TV," *Court TV Crime Library*, chapter 6, n.d., <http://www.crimelibrary.com/gangsters_outlaws/cops_others/clarence_gideon> (May 4, 2007).

4. Lewis, p. 245.

5. "Case Background."

6. Lewis, p. 64.

7. "Case Background."

8. Lewis, p. 101.

9. Ibid., pp. 71, 77–78.

10. David W. Rintels, *Gideon's Trumpet*, Hallmark Hall of Fame Productions, 1980.

11. Ibid.

12. "40 years: *Gideon* v. *Wainwright*," State of Connecticut Division of Public Defender Services Web site, n.d., <http://www.ocpd.state.ct.us/Content/Gideon/Gideon.htm> (May 4, 2007).

13. Clarence Earl Gideon, Petition for Writ of Certorari, June 5, 1962, p. 3, Landmark Supreme Court Cases Web site, n.d., <http://www.landmarkcases.org/gideon/gideon.pdf> (November 18, 2006).

14. Lewis, p. 77.

 **A Gambler Tries to Beat the Odds**

1. Anthony Lewis, *Gideon's Trumpet* (New York: Random House, 1963, 1980), p. 102.

2. Ibid., p. 23.

3. Clarence Earl Gideon, Petition for Writ of Certorari, June 5, 1962, p. 3, Landmark Supreme Court Cases Web site, n.d., <http://www.landmarkcases.org/gideon/gideon.pdf> (November 18, 2006).

4. Ibid.

5. Lewis, p. 8.

6. Gideon, p. 3.

7. Lewis, p. 9.

8. Ibid.

9. Ibid., pp. 27, 36.

10. David W. Rintels, *Gideon's Trumpet,* Hallmark Hall of Fame Productions, 1980.

11. Bernard Schwartz, *Decision: How the Supreme Court Decides Cases* (New York: Oxford University Press, 1996.), p. 111.

## 4 Before the Highest Court

1. Bruce R. Jacob, "Memories and Reflections About *Gideon v. Wainwright*," *Stetson Law Review*, Fall 2003, vol. 23, no.1, p. 224.

2. Anthony Lewis, *Gideon's Trumpet* (New York: Random House, 1964, 1980), p. 151.

3. Ibid., p. 155.

4. John B. Taylor, *The Right to Counsel and Privilege against Self-Incrimination* (Santa Barbara, Calif.: ABC-CLIO, 2004), p. 63.

5. Ibid.

6. Lewis, p. 165.

7. *Gideon v. Wainwright* oral arguments transcript, January 15, 1963, p. 25, <http://www.rashkind.com/gideon/Gideon_v_%20Wainwright_oral_argument.transcript.htm> (April 4, 2008).

8. Ibid., p. 168.

9. Taylor, p. 64.

10. Lewis, p. 141.

11. Ibid., pp. 141–143.

12. David Krajicek, "A Florida Burglary, review of the case on Court TV," *Court TV Crime Library*, chapter 7, n.d., <http://www.crimelibrary.com/gangsters_outlaws/cops_others/clarence_gideon> (May 4, 2007).

13. David W. Rintels, *Gideon's Trumpet*, Hallmark Hall of Fame Productions, 1980.

14. *Gideon* v. *Wainwright* oral arguments transcript, p. 9.

15. Krajicek.

16. Lewis, pp. 181–182.

17. Rintels.

18. Lewis, p. 179.

19. Ibid., p. 181.

20. *Gideon* v. *Wainwright* oral arguments transcript, pp. 24, 26, 32.

21. Lewis, p. 187.

22. Krajicek.

23. *Gideon* v. *Wainwright* oral arguments transcript, p. 36.

24. Lewis, p. 192.

25. Taylor, p. 58.

26. Bernard Schwartz, *Decision: How the Supreme Court Decides Cases* (New York: Oxford University Press, 1996), p. 112.

27. Krajicek.

28. Hugo Black, Supreme Court Decision in *Gideon* v. *Wainwright*, 372 U.S. 335 (1963), section II, Para 7, FindLaw Web site, n.d., <http://caselaw.lp.findlaw.com/cgi-bin/getcase.pl?court=US&vol=372&invol=335> (April 27, 2007).

29. 372 U.S. 335 (1963), section II, Para 2.

30. 372 U.S. 335 (1963), section II, Para 7.

 **5** ## Not Over Yet: Gideon's New Trial

1. Anthony Lewis, *Gideon's Trumpet* (New York: Random House, 1964, 1980), pp. 234–235.

2. David Krajicek, "A Florida Burglary, review of the case on Court TV," *Court TV Crime Library*, chapter 9, n.d.,

<http://www.crimelibrary.com/gangsters_outlaws/cops_others/ clarence_gideon> (May 4, 2007).

3. Lewis, p. 235.
4. Ibid.
5. Ibid.
6. Ibid.
7. Ibid., p. 165.
8. David W. Rintels, *Gideon's Trumpet*, Hallmark Hall of Fame Productions, 1980.
9. Lewis, p. 241.
10. Rintels.
11. Krajicek.
12. Clarence Earl Gideon, Petition for Writ of Certorari, June 5, 1962, p. 3, Landmark Supreme Court Cases Web site, n.d., <http://www.landmarkcases.org/gideon/gideon.pdf> (November 18, 2006).
13. Lewis, p. 244.
14. Krajicek, chapter 1.
15. "Case Background," *Gideon at 40: Understanding the Right to Counsel*, p. 2, National Association of Criminal Defense Lawyers Web site, n.d., <http://www.nacdl.org/gideon> (November 12, 2006).
16. Lewis, pp. 245–246.
17. Bruce R. Jacob, "Memories and Reflections About *Gideon* v. *Wainwright*," *Stetson Law Review*, Fall 2003, vol. 23, no.1, p. 270.
18. Lewis, p. 246.
19. Jacob.
20. Lewis, p. 250.

## 6 Watching History Unfold

1. Stephen Murray, "Outstanding Courtroom Drama" (review of *Gideon's Trumpet* starring Henry Fonda), April 24, 2002, <http://www.epinions.com/content_62120365700> (May 4, 2007).

2. David W. Rintels, *Gideon's Trumpet*, Hallmark Hall of Fame Productions, 1980.
3. Ibid.
4. Ibid.
5. Ibid.
6. Ibid.
7. Murray, p. 1.
8. Rintels.
9. Ibid.
10. Bruce R. Jacob, "Memories and Reflections About *Gideon* v. *Wainwright*," *Stetson Law Review*, Fall 2003, vol. 23, no.1, p. 272.
11. Rintels.
12. David Krajicek, "A Florida Burglary, review of the case on Court TV," *Court TV Crime Library*, chapter 10, n.d., <http://www.crimelibrary.com/gangsters_outlaws/cops_others/ clarence_gideon> (May 4, 2007).
13. Jacob, p. 295.

 **7** **The Promise of** *Gideon*

1. John B. Taylor, *The Right to Counsel and Privilege Against Self-Incrimination* (Santa Barbara, Calif: ABC-CLIO, 2004), p. 67.
2. Ibid., pp. 67–68.
3. Anthony Lewis, *Gideon's Trumpet* (New York: Random House, 1964, 1980), p. 212.
4. "40 Years: *Gideon* v. *Wainwright*," State of Connecticut Division of Public Defender Services Web site, n.d., <http://www.ocpd.state.ct.us/Content/Gideon/Gideon.htm> (May 4, 2007).
5. Taylor, p. 68.
6. Lewis, p. 215.
7. Ibid., p. 205.
8. Ibid., p. 208.
9. Ibid., pp. 207–210.
10. Ibid., p. 209.

11. "40 Years: *Gideon* v. *Wainwright*."

12. Lewis, p. 207.

13. "40 Years: *Gideon* v. *Wainwright*," ("Letter from U.S. Senator Joseph Lieberman").

14. Rita A. Fry, "*Gideon* at Forty: The Promise Comes With a Price Tag," *NLADA Cornerstone*, vol. 24, no. 4, Winter 2002–2003.

15. Ted Gest, "One Poor Man's Legacy," *U. S. News and World Report*, vol. 114, no. 11, March 22, 1993, p. 19.

16. David Krajicek, "A Florida Burglary, review of the case on Court TV," *Court TV Crime Library*, chapter 10, n.d., <http://www.crimelibrary.com/gangsters_outlaws/cops_others/ clarence_gideon> (May 4, 2007).

17. Joshua C. Krumholz, "In Defense of the Indigent," *The Recorder*, October 28, 2005, retrieved November 3, 2006 via Thomson-Gale General Reference Center Gold database.

18. Edward M. Kennedy, "What 'Gideon' Promised," *Legal Times*, March 28, 2003, <http://www.nacdl.org/public.nsf/ GideonAnniversary/news10?opendocument> (January 3, 2008).

19. Ibid.

20. Leonardo Castro, "Commentary: 'Gideon' turns 40— a look at the case, and its future," *Minnesota Lawyer*, March 24, 2003, retrieved November 3, 2006, via Thomson-Gale General Business File database.

21. Krumholz.

**acquitted**—To be cleared of a charge; set free; after consideration of evidence, the judgment that a defendant is not guilty of the crime as charged.

*amicus curiae*—Literally, "friend of the court." An *amicus curiae* brief is a written response from a person or institution not personally involved in a case that supports a particular side.

**Bill of Rights**—The first ten amendments to the U.S. Constitution guaranteeing basic rights and liberties to all citizens of the United States.

**capital case**—A case in which the possible sentence is the death penalty or life imprisonment.

**circuit court**—A court whose judges hold (or used to hold) trials in various locations, in order to cover an entire district.

**cross-examination**—Questioning of a witness who has already testified, conducted by the attorney for the opposing side.

**defendant**—A person who is accused of a crime or violation or sued in a court of law.

**double jeopardy**—Trying a person a second time for an offense he or she was acquitted of in a previous trial. The Fifth Amendment to the U.S. Constitution prohibits this.

**felony**—A crime more serious than a misdemeanor, usually punishable by incarceration for over a year in a state correctional facility or by death.

**incarcerate**—To confine; place in prison.

**indigent**—Without money, poor; living in poverty.

***in forma pauperis***—Literally, "in the manner of a pauper." Permission given to a poor person to proceed in a case without paying required fees and court costs.

**larceny**—Stealing, theft.

**litigant**—A person involved in a lawsuit.

**misdemeanor**—Misconduct; breaking the criminal law, not as serious as a felony.

**peremptory challenge**—Dismissal of a potential juror by either side without giving a reason.

**petition**—A written request directed to a court.

**precedent**—A judicial decision used as a standard in future similar cases.

**public defender**—A lawyer who provides representation to indigent people accused of crimes; often part of a public or private nonprofit organization that includes support staff.

**public defense system**—A method of providing criminal defense services to those accused of a crime who cannot afford to hire an attorney.

**rebuttal**—A legal argument contradicting another statement.

**verdict**—The decision of the judge or jury on a case based on evidence and testimony.

**writ**—A formal written order issued by a court of law directing something to be done or not done.

**writ of certiorari**—An order of an appellate court declaring whether it will hear an appeal from a lower court; if the writ is denied, the higher court will not hear the case; if the writ is granted, the higher court will hear the case and order the lower court to send the case records for review.

**writ of habeas corpus**—A formal order requiring a prisoner to be brought into court or before a judge to determine whether he or she is being held lawfully.

# FURTHER READING

Campbell, Andrea. *Rights of the Accused.* Philadelphia: Chelsea House Publishers, 2001.

Compston, Christine L. *Earl Warren: Justice for All.* Oxford and New York: Oxford University Press, 2001.

Freedman, Russell. *In Defense of Liberty: The Story of America's Bill of Rights.* New York: Holiday House, 2003.

Fridell, Ron. *Gideon v. Wainwright: The Right to Free Counsel.* Tarrytown, N.Y.: Marshall Cavendish Benchmark, 2007.

Horn, Geoffrey M. *The Supreme Court.* Milwaukee, Wisc.: World Almanac Library, 2003.

Lewis, Anthony. *Gideon's Trumpet.* New York: Random House, 1963.

Taylor, John B. *The Right to Counsel and Privilege Against Self-Incrimination.* Santa Barbara, Calif.: ABC-CLIO, 2004.

# INTERNET ADDRESSES

**Audio clips of oral arguments in *Gideon* v. *Wainwright***
<http://www.oyez.org/oyez/resource/case/139/audiore sources>

**David Krajicek, "A Florida Burglary," Court TV Crime Library**
<http://www.crimelibrary.com/gangsters_outlaws/ cops_others/clarence_gideon/index.html>

**The Internet Movie Database: *Gideon's Trumpet***
<http://www.imdb.com/title/tt0080789/>

**Landmark Supreme Court Cases Web site**
<http://www.landmarkcases.org/gideon/home.html>

# INDEX